TRAINS

By Seymour Reit
Illustrated by Tom LaPadula

A Golden Book • New York
Western Publishing Company, Inc., Racine, Wisconsin 53404

Library of Congress Catalog Card Number: 89-81961 ISBN: 0-307-17869-2/ISBN: 0-307-67869-5 (lib. bdg.)   A B C D E F G H I J K L M

Long ago, when people wanted to travel farther than they could walk, they had to ride on horses or in wagons and coaches. All these methods of travel proved to be bumpy, uncomfortable, and slow. Everyone wanted a better way to travel across the land. Finally, in the early 1800's, men built railroads.

The first trains had passenger cars that looked just like the old coaches. This train, which was used over 150 years ago, was named the *DeWitt Clinton*. It traveled on railroad tracks between different cities in New York State.

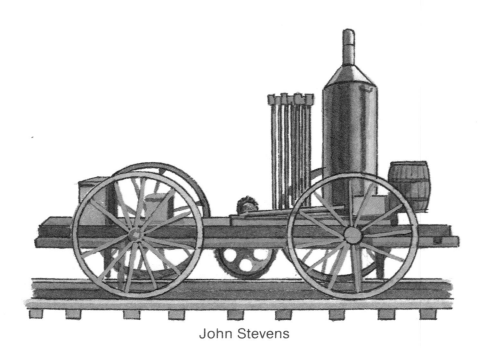

John Stevens

George Washington

The engine that pulls the whole train is called a locomotive. The first locomotives had tall smokestacks and big iron boilers. Water in the boilers made steam, and the steam turned the train's wheels.

Early locomotives came in many different shapes and sizes. And they all had names.

Henry Campbell

Buffalo

Many locomotives had big iron bumpers on their front. These bumpers, called cowcatchers, helped to keep the tracks clear of wandering animals by gently pushing them aside.

The first trains were not very fast. One day there was a famous race between a horse and a locomotive. The locomotive was named the *Tom Thumb*. The horse ran on tracks next to the train and pulled a car filled with passengers.

The race was very close. First the horse was ahead. Then the locomotive was ahead. And finally…the horse won!

During the early days of railroads, trains often got bogged down in heavy snow. Then the passengers had to get off and help shovel the snow away.

This locomotive blows the snow off the tracks with a giant machine called a rotary steam snow shovel.

When the railroads spread out to the West, they met another kind of trouble. Some Indian tribes hated the noisy monsters, which they called iron horses. They didn't want more people coming to the West. The Indians feared that trains would ruin their beautiful prairie lands. Sometimes the Indians attacked the trains and tried to drive them from the rails.

But nothing could stop the great iron horses. Trains were here to stay.

Riding in trains was much more comfortable than riding in bumpy, bouncy horse-driven coaches. As trains became more advanced they included private railroad cars for the very rich. The private cars looked like beautiful rooms. They had big armchairs, fancy carpets on the floor, and lace curtains at the windows.

A man named George Pullman invented a special car
that had berths—places where people could sleep. He
also designed cars where hungry travelers could have
meals.

Pullman's dining cars looked like fine restaurants.
The waiters wore spotless uniforms. The tables had
white cloths and were set with crystal glasses and silver
knives, forks, and spoons. All the food was cooked in a
small galley at one end of the long dining car.

Today there are very few steam locomotives still in use. Most trains now run on diesel fuel or on electric power. Trains also ride smoother and are longer and faster than ever before.

Trains carry many things. They carry people, and also goods such as cars and clothes, milk and mail, toys and TV sets, books and blue jeans. Shiny railroad tracks crisscross the land, linking us all together.

The locomotive of this freight train runs on diesel fuel. It pulls a long line of cars filled with different products.

The locomotive of this passenger train runs on electric power. It pulls a long line of cars filled with travelers.

Everyone's train trip begins at a railroad station. This is the place where passengers buy their tickets and get information about different trains. The railroad station is also the place where people can check their baggage and buy snacks and magazines for the journey.

Some railroad stations are big and some are small. But in each of them, travelers wait to hear the exciting call: "ALL ABOARD!"

13 - 25

TO GATES 26 - 38

TO
CONCOURSE
AND
TRAINS

TICKET OFFICE

TRAINS	NO.	DEP.	ARR.
STAMET	15	1:11	1:31
ESSEX	12	2:04	2:21
MOSLER	27	6:51	7:20
HOPEWELL	2	7:01	9:41
BEACON	34	8:11	10:11

Passenger cars, or coaches, are comfortable and
clean. There are big windows so people can enjoy the
view as the train moves. There are lights so passengers
can read at night.

Some passenger trains have spaces called compartments. These are private little rooms. Each compartment has its own seats and a tiny bathroom. There is also a clothes closet. At night the seats can be turned down to make comfortable beds.

Some trains have mail cars. Sorting out letters and postcards while the train speeds along helps to save the post office valuable time.

Many trains also have baggage cars. This is where big suitcases, trunks, and heavy boxes can be stored safely during a long journey.

The snack car is a special car where people can buy things to eat. Snack cars usually have foods such as sandwiches and cakes, cookies and milk, fruit juice and soft drinks.

It's fun to ride in the observation car! This car is for sightseeing. It has big picture windows and sometimes a curved glass roof called a bubble dome.

People begin and end their trips at a railroad station. But goods begin and end their rides at a freight yard. In a big freight yard there are many tracks and rail sidings. There are different cars for carrying different products. And there are huge cranes that help workmen to load and unload things.

Freight trains are made up of many different kinds of railroad cars, all linked together.

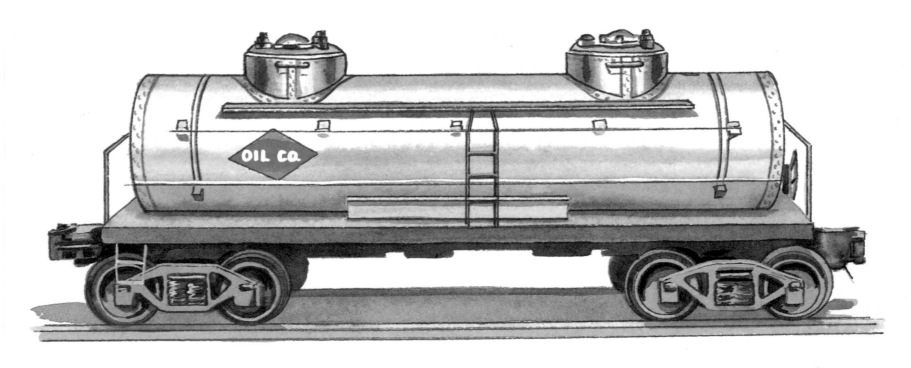

Tank cars are built for carrying liquids such as oil, gasoline, and chemicals.

Boxcars carry all kinds of factory goods such as furniture, television sets, shoes, clothes, and dishwashers.

Livestock cars are made to carry animals such as cows, pigs, sheep, and chickens.

Hopper cars are very strong. They are made to hold coal, sand, iron ore, and crushed gravel.

An auto rack is a special kind of freight car. It is a flatcar built for carrying new automobiles from the factory to cities where they will be sold. The auto rack flatcar has three different levels. It can carry twelve or more automobiles at the same time.

8074

Some flatcars are called piggybacks because they carry whole trailers, piggyback style. The trailers are tied to the flatcars. At the end of the trip they are connected to truck cabs and driven away.

The flatcars can also carry shipping containers packed with products. The heavy metal containers are loaded on the flatcars by giant cranes.

Refrigerator cars carry items that must be kept cold while traveling. They are used for foods such as milk, butter, eggs, and cheese.

The last car on a freight train is called a caboose. The train conductor's office is in this little car, which may also have bunks for the train crew.

Railroad tracks go everywhere, crisscrossing the country. Tracks not only go around mountains, but also through them in man-made tunnels. Tunnels can also be found under wide rivers. Inside the tunnels there are lights that help the train's motorman to see the tracks up ahead.

Trains sometimes come to big rivers or deep valleys as they speed along. They cross over them on special railroad bridges that have tracks. The first railroad bridges were built of wood. But now they're made of iron and steel, or out of stone blocks.

This bridge is called a trestle bridge. It is made of strong steel girders.

Passenger trains carry people. Freight trains carry products. But there are other kinds of trains that are used for special purposes.

In some places there are very steep hills, so people ride in cogwheel trains. A cogwheel train has an extra wheel with steel teeth. These teeth work a little like the zippers on our clothes. They hook on a special track that helps the train as it goes uphill.

Another unusual kind of train is the cable car. Cable cars are pulled along the tracks by strong metal ropes called cables. Many cable cars travel through the air, pulled along by cables attached to high towers. This kind of train is often found in theme parks.

Big cities are very crowded. The streets are filled with people, cars, trucks, and buses, and there isn't any room for railroad trains. But in some cities trains run on tracks built high above the busy streets. This type of train is called an elevated railway or el for short. In the United States the busiest els are in Chicago.

Some big cities have subway trains that speed along in tunnels far below the crowded streets. Subway travel is a fast and easy way for city people to get places. Boston, Chicago, New York, and Washington, D.C., all have subway systems. Many big cities in Europe also have subway trains.

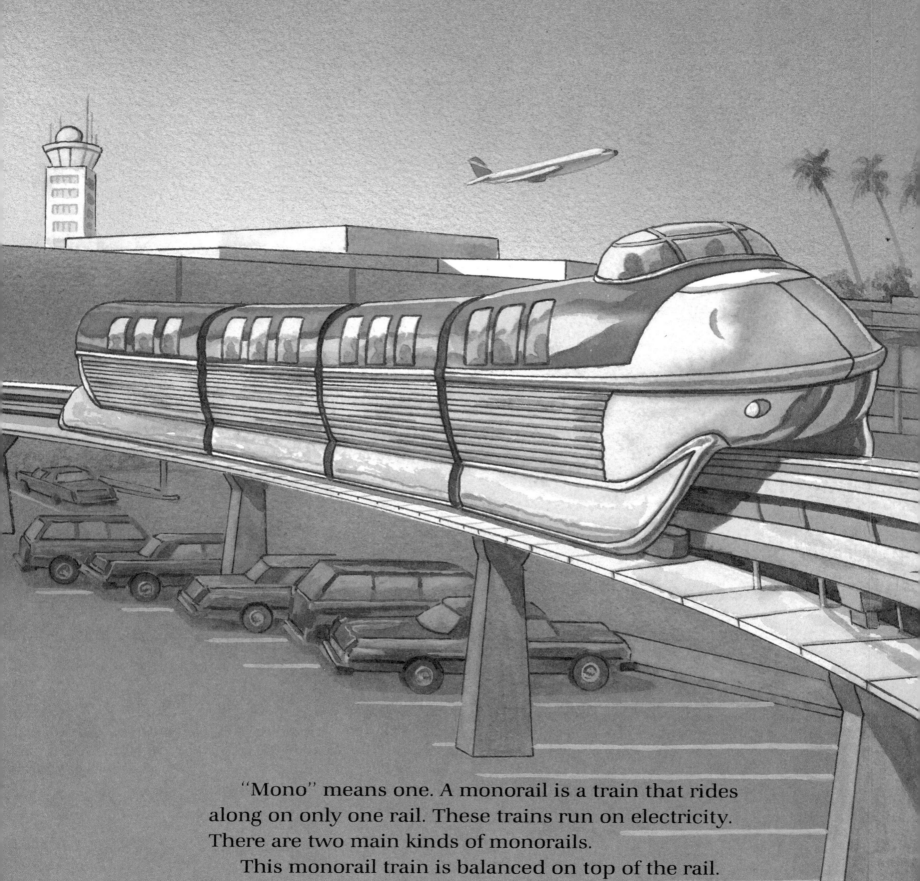

"Mono" means one. A monorail is a train that rides
along on only one rail. These trains run on electricity.
There are two main kinds of monorails.

This monorail train is balanced on top of the rail.
It is built on towers high above the ground.

This monorail train hangs below the rail. Many airports and amusement parks have monorails.

Stand back.
Clear the track.
Watch the high-speed
 trains whiz by!

Here they come.
There they go.
As fast as you can
 blink an eye!

With better engines and smoother rails, trains now race along faster than ever before. This is the French TGV super-speed passenger train. It can go more than 200 miles an hour.

This famous train speeds along in Japan. It is the *Shinkansen* and is so fast, people call it the bullet train.

Railroads have certainly come a long, long way since the day the tiny locomotive *Tom Thumb* lost a race with a galloping horse!